1.

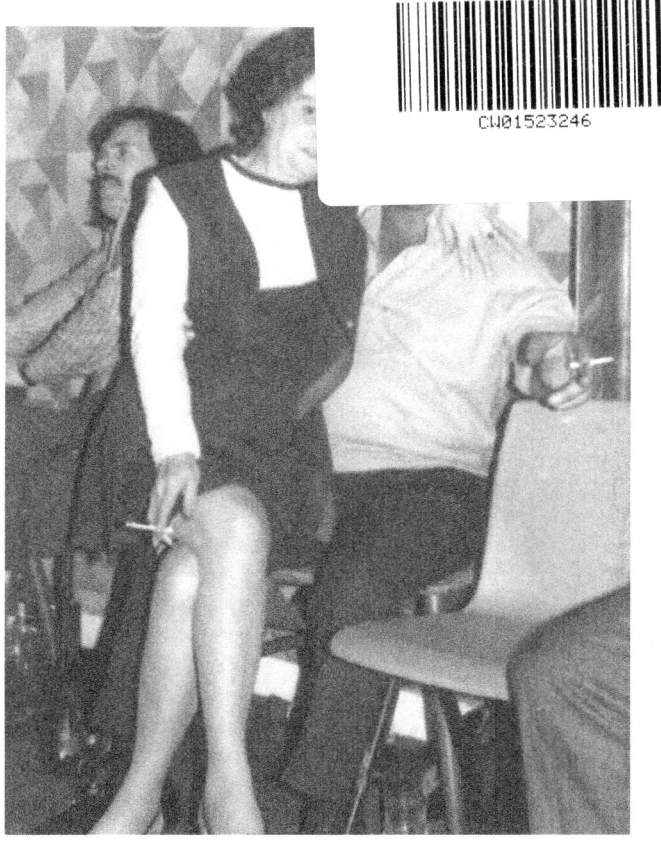

I would like to dedicate this book to my Mum and Dad.

They were an inspiration and I learned how to live through their love and constant support. Thank you for always being here.

A LIGHT WITHIN

by Margaret Coletta

Introduction

To me, Glasgow is a home with a warm feeling, and the atmosphere is terrific. Everybody likes the Scots, or so they tell us. Glasgow has always seemed to me to be a friendly place, a place where I was born, where I grew up and where I still live.

I was born in the late 1950's which was a time of poverty, and there wasn't a lot of community activity, although there were lots of happy times with family. Grandparents often stayed with the sons and daughters. My family were seven siblings and my parents, but we still had room for my Italian Grandad when he couldn't live on his own, after my gran passed. There was love and connection.

Before my Mum, Dad, two older brothers, two older sisters, my younger sister and I moved to Easterhouse, we lived in Duke St in Glasgow in a one bedroom bedsit. It was a bit of a squeeze but was quite common for working class people in the city. We didn't have a lot of money or material things and times in the fifties and sixties were really hard. My mum and dad always provided for us as much as they could, and my dad worked all the hours he could while my mum looked after all of us.

So, that was that. It was my mum that looked after us and then when my dad came home from work my mum would make dinner. That was daily life for the most part and with me being a toddler at the time I can't remember if my older siblings helped my mum in the house. My mum did all the housework, cooking, cleaning and all the shopping. The family roles were quite traditional and it seemed to work, for us at least. There was another tradition for many in Glasgow where the man worked all week and drank all weekend, but my dad was a real family man with strong roots in his own family and the traditions of his parents. They were Italians, but I'll come to that a wee bit later.

We didn't have any carpets, and I don't think that was an interior design decision but a financial one, we had vinyl instead, slippy linoleum. We also had a coal fire which was great, warm and homely. I loved the smells and watching the coals burning, the simple things in life: heat, light and a loving home. We had an old black and white tv and it was one of those where my mum and dad had to put money into the back of the tv for it to come on to make sure we could watch the programs that we all liked. Sometimes the telly would 'conk out' meaning there wasn't any money in it and we've have to shout, "Mum, the telly's conked out!"

My mum and dad would watch the soaps like, Coronation street, Emmerdale and Crossroads; we watched the cartoons, like Tom & Jerry, Popeye, Skippy the bush kangaroo and my favourite Topogigio. I also had a bendy toy called Rupert the bear, another favourite cartoon character.

After a few years here, when I was about four, my mum & dad then got word of moving to a new house in Easterhouse. At that time 'the scheme' was just getting built, but later came to be known as one of the biggest housing estates in Glasgow and also in the UK. It also became well known for other reasons like poverty, gangs and other social problems, but I was a toddler and untouched by this. The little light of happiness and hope burned steadily within me in the safe environment of a loving family home. Easterhouse was mostly tenement buildings, six families in each block. We had three bedrooms, a kitchen, a bathroom and a living room. There were a lot of fields where our new house was.

Because I would have been four years old at this time it wouldn't be long before I'd be starting school when I was 5. My mum and dad thought this new house was amazing! We all did because we didn't have as many rooms before, and we didn't even have a separate kitchen or an inside bathroom in our house in Duke St. This was luxury! An inside toilet and a ceramic bath not like the tin one we had before. This was posh for us! The Ritz! When we moved to Easterhouse it was so nice to have all this space. As I said, yes there were gangs that used to fight over at the pitches; they had weird names like' The Drummie' and 'The Den Toy' but we would never see anything. We were safe and protected. I would just hear my brothers and sisters talking about it the next day, or if my mum was speaking to one of the other neighbours about it. Easterhouse got a bad name because of this, but no matter where gangs were fighting or where you stayed it was always Easterhouse that got the bad name. The new scheme with big hopes and vision for the future wasn't turning out the way people had dreamed.

Though we had much more space, I still had to share a room with my three sisters; my two brothers shared a room and my mum and dad had 'the big room' of the house.

4.

Even though we had a bigger house it didn't mean my mum and dad had a lot more money.Times were still hard. But at least we had vinyl and a rug to sit at the coal fire and watch the telly. Life was simple, but through the eyes of a happy child it was good. We often had power cuts in those days and sometimes there would even be a bread shortage because some of the bread factories went on strike. Other items like milk and eggs could also be scarce. When you went to get certain groceries you were only allowed one loaf, six eggs and one pint of milk. So it was still tough but my mum and dad always did their best to provide for us, that was enough.

When we first lived in Easterhouse my dad worked in Partick at Robertsons scrap yard. He would put old cars, vans and lorries in this big machine and it would bash it all down to flatten it like a box size. Amazing! My mum still didn't work at this time as I was just about to start school and my wee sister, who was the youngest, would only be three years old at this time.

My mum and dad were amazing people to me, my role models, my protectors, my providers and sometimes even my friends. They were kind, thoughtful and caring; they had a very good nature and of course they would have disagreements but they would never fall out and not speak to each other. If I ever saw my mum looking sad after a heated disagreement with my Dad, then felt a little bit sad. I really didn't like to see my mum upset. Even though I was young I would sometimes ask my mum "what's wrong?" But she would only say "Nothing, I'm okay." And *it would* be ok, they would always sort it out one way or another. I feel so grateful to have grown up in a home where there was the love of two parents. This was a good foundation for a happy life.

As I mentioned, my dad's parents were Italian and came over from Italy in the early 1930's to have a better life. Even though my grandparents were Italian my dad was born in Scotland, for what I can remember(as I was still quite young) my grandparents opened 'a chippy' a fish and chip shop, and they lived directly above the shop. It became a well known chip shop in the area and people from all over the East end of Glasgow came for the popular fish and chips as well as everything else that they did, like battered chicken, battered sausages and fritters. Everything was battered in Glasgow, even the people sometimes!

My mum and dad met in the Army and they were only in their teens. My dad was a little bit older than my mum,. When my mum used to tell us how they met she was also quick to let us know that she didn't really like the army. One time when she was on leave she didn't go back so the army sent out the military police to come and get her from my grandad's house, her dad's. She got arrested and it wasn't long after that my mum left the army, though she was still in touch with my dad and after seeing him for a while they eventually got married. They began their married lives in Duke St. My younger brother Mario was the only one of the siblings born in Easterhouse and this was when my mum was in her early 40's. I remember one time when my Auntie Margaret was visiting and as she was going home she said to my mum, "You will be fine, don't worry." This was because my mum wanted to have my wee brother Mario in the house, but the Doctor's advised her not to do this because of my her age. They were worried in case any complications set in. Looking back, I am so glad that the Doctor's said this to my mum, because when my brother was born he wasn't breathing and it was the doctors and nurses that saved his life. I am just so grateful that we have a National Health service who do an amazing job; even to this day I am so thankful for everything that the NHS does. When my mum and my wee brother came home it was great to have a wee brother to look after and to take out for walks. I can remember we had a dog at the time who was called 'Bruno' and he would come with us for a walk and when we would stop he would sit under the pram and guard my wee brother. He was a brilliant dog, I loved him so much. So, my earliest years were a happy time, a safe time, a loving time. Let me tell you a little more.

The Light Within

Chapter 1

New Beginnings

Well, where does one start on the journey through so many memories. So many beginnings and some sad endings, but let me begin with school, as this was quite an unusual adventure for me.

Well, my first day starting school is one that I will never forget as long as I live. I can see it as if it was yesterday, My primary school was called *St Claire's* and we didn't stay far from the school. In fact, it was walking distance even for someone as small as me! So, on my first day I was a bit upset because I had always been with my mum since I was born as we didn't have any nurseries in those days when I was a toddler. As my mum left me at school even my mum was upset at the thought of me going into school crying, but I was ok once I got into the class. I can still remember my teacher was 'a big lady', she was not unlike Mrs.Doubtfire in build and looks. Her name was Mrs Milligan and as she was making sure all of the children were getting settled into the class she sat us all down at our desk where we got a pencil, a jotter and a reading book which was called Jane and John. Not long after this, after a short time of the teacher telling us about school, a bell rang and we all went out. Because we were outside I assumed that it was time to go home. I felt quite happy and relieved that my first day had been pretty quick and relatively painless. So, naturally I went home and as it was only walking distance I knew the way. I got in the house and my mum said,
"Who's that?"
I replied happily and as if it was quite obvious said, 'it's me'
This was a common response when we had been out playing and when we were coming in or out we were always to shout, 'It's me', but my mum with a curious frown asked,
"What are you doing home?"
I said, stating what seemed pretty clear to me, "We were all out so I came home."
Well, my mum was not exactly happy that I had came home and she said to me,
"When the bell goes it's only play time, for you to play with the other girls and boys that are out playing and then you go back into class then the bell goes again."
How was I supposed to know that? Nobody told me! One minute we were in, and the next minute we were out. "Time to go home", I thought.

Well, it didn't end here. My mum marched me back up to school, probably more embarrassed than angry, and as she got there the teachers were all looking for me. My mum said to the teacher that I thought it was time to come home and told me to say sorry because of *'the trouble I caused'* with me going home. Nobody told me! I know it mightn't have been funny, for the teachers who had lost a child on the first day, my mum who had to return an escapee child on the first day, and even for me, having to apologise and feel bad about going home. Well, maybe my mum had a laugh about it later on with my Dad and her pals, thinking 'Margaret had enough after an hour of school.' After all, didn't she go missing from the army when she got the chance. Like mother like daughter I think. Despite, *the trouble I caused* it's a beautiful memory for me and one that still makes me laugh.

St Claire's school was brilliant! I did enjoy playing with my friends and we would play, 'Cheese', skipping ropes, and we would 'Tig' each other and run away. The time I had there was great but then I started having trouble with my reading and I couldn't pronounce some of the words. So, my Headteacher gave me a letter to give to my mum and dad to say that the school wanted to speak to them. My mum came up to the school to meet with the Headteacher and my classroom teacher Mrs. Milligan. It was basically to tell my mum that I was *behind* with my reading and having problems with my speech when I was trying to pronounce some of the words. The Headteacher said to my mum that I would need to go to *a special school*, this was the name for a special needs school in those days. My mum said,

"Well I need to speak to my husband when he comes in from work."

When my dad came in from work he said to my mum,

"How did you get on at the school and what did the teachers want?"
My mum told my dad about *the trouble* I was having with my reading and my speech and that I would have to go to *a special school* which would be St Kenneth's in Blackhill, which was further away and not within walking distance. My dad said,

"How's she going to get there and get back home?"
My mum replied,

"There's a *special school bus* that will pick the wain up and bring her back home. She'll need to see a speech therapist as well but they'll come to the school to see her and will use one of the offices."

8.

My mum and dad gently and clearly explained to me what was happening but I started to get a bit upset because I wouldn't see my friends at St Claires. I was pretty sad at first because I couldn't really understand why I had to leave my friends and go somewhere new on my own, which was far away, and I'd need to get a bus!
My first day when I was to start St Kenneth's, just before the bus came for me, my mum could see I was a bit anxious so tried to reassure me, though I wasn't completely reassured!

"You'll be ok… you will meet new friends."

When the bus came for me I went on and I was the only passenger at first. But then the driver went to pick up the other kids from were they stayed, and the bus started to get a little busier, but not too hectic. As the bus passed other children going to their own school they shouted names at the bus as we stopped to pick up other kids. And when I looked at them shouting they would shout, "Speckie!" to me and "Four eyes." At first, I was really upset by this, but by the time I got to the school I felt a tiny bit better. But it was cruel and it was sore. I know that children don't think about how cruel words can be to another but the old chant of 'sticks and stones can break my bones but names will never hurt me' is just not true. When you're a small child, words hurt.

My new Headteacher was called Mrs Johnston and my teacher was a nun, Sister Mary. She was from a Catholic organisation called 'The Daughters of Charity', which is a branch of the St Vincent De Paul. They were so nice to me. Sister Mary was the only nun in our school and she always had time to listen to me and help me to do my reading. She took the time to listen and to help with my reading. I didn't feel like I was 'trouble' or a problem to be solved, but just a child who needed a little support. When I had my reading at St Claires, I felt more relaxed and I never really felt like that at my first school. Maybe the time for extra support wasn't possible at a bigger school but when my teacher was doing my reading with me there, it felt as if I couldn't do it. Maybe this was the reason I *fell behind;* too much stress and feeling like I was failing and trouble seemed to make the 'problem' worse. But I began to really enjoy my new primary school and I met new friends. I still see some of them in the passing to this day and we often say hello to each other.

I can remember when we got PE(Physical Education), and we had to wear plimsols, simple black cotton shoes with a rubber soul. No Adidas or Nike required! They were brilliant and I really liked them because everyone wore the same and there was no competition. As I started my speech therapy lessons I was very shy and it took me quite a while to get used to the therapist, she was called Mrs Stewart. It was mostly all women teachers in my school. In fact, I think there was only two male teachers; this was normal I think for primary teaching in those days. As time went on my reading started to improve and my therapy lessons were progressing quite well. Words that I couldn't pronounce before were starting to feel easier and I slowly but surely became a bit more comfortable at reading. My confidence was a bit fragile though as I still didn't want to read out in class incase I made a mistake, and I worried that some of the others might laugh at me. When Sister Mary gently asked,

"Why do you not want to read out in class Margaret?"

I said to her,

"If I make a mistake I don't want the other girls and boys to laugh at me."

She said that would not happen and encouraged me to try. So I did and it was ok. When it was time to go home and back on the bus there were quite a few of us but we all stayed in different parts of Easterhouse. So, I was always the last one to get off and again I was called names when I got off the bus. When I got into the house my mum saw that I was crying and she said,

"What's wrong? Did something happen in school?"

I said,

"No, school was good, its when I came off the school bus I was getting called names again."

My mum tried to comfort me and also make me toughen a bit and said,

"Och, don't bother with them. I will come with you in the morning and wait till you're on the bus, and then I'll meet you coming off the bus when you come home."

10.

I felt much better that my mum would be with me. My friends who I met at St Claire's would still come up for me to go out and play and we would play 'kick-the-can', 'red lights' and 'chap door run away', but sometimes we would get caught! The neighbours would tell my mum and she would give me a telling off and they would go to my pals mum's as well and tell on them. And that wasn't the end of it! My mum then told my dad when he got home and I got *another* telling off. My dad wasn't happy about it and said if I did it again I would get kept in and not get out to play. But my pals and I still did it! Are children not supposed to break the rules and test the boundaries sometimes? I thought so. But we had to be more careful, or skilful and make sure we didn't get caught.

On a Sunday my mum would take us to mass but sometimes my dad would work. My mum would take us by herself and at that time they had just built St Clare's Church beside the school. We had two nuns from *the Daughters of Charity* and we had priest called Father Jim from the *Salesians of Don Bosco*. They were really brilliant and brought so much to the Church, and to the community in Easterhouse. They started up a club during the week for all the kids to go when you came home from school. We had games like 'snakes and ladders' and drawing, and then juice and a biscuit. On the Monday when we would go back into school Sister Mary would ask us,

"Who went to mass yesterday?"

A few of us put our hands up so she said,

"Who can tell me the colour of vestments that the Priest had on?"

I put my hand up and said what colour he had on, then she asked some of the others why they did not go to mass? They usually said their mum and dad slept in or some of them just didn't go, so Sr Mary said,

"Maybe you can ask your mum and dad to take you next week."

When I came home from school I would always get changed, and usually go down *the back court* where my pals would be playing football. I played with them as well and it was great fun. It was always a really good atmosphere and we had so much fun, usually. But there was one time when one of the boys wouldn't pass the ball, so I shouted to him,

11.

"Pass the ball!"

He said 'No!" and ran away with the ball, so I ran after him and he ran all the way home with and I chased him. Eventually I caught him, even though the game was well and truly finished I said to him,

"You need to pass the ball."

So I took the ball off him. Someone had to tell him! He did come back to finish the game off. Another time, when I was about eight years old I had to go into hospital to get my tonsils out as I always took sore throats. The doctor said to my mum that I had to get them out. When I was in hospital it was pretty good because I got ice cream and jelly. Thank God for tonsillitis! I said to my mum,

" I don't want to come home."

My mum was taken aback and said,

"You need to come home but you'll be off school for a few days."

I was never off school and this was the very first time. As I was off for a few days the school sent *the school board* out even though they knew what was wrong and why I was off. Once again, thank God for tonsillitis! Ice cream, jelly and a few days off school. Brilliant! A few months later my wee sister and I were playing *down the back* with the bike as we shared a bike because it cost a lot for my mum and dad; they would give us what they could afford. So, it was my turn and I said,

"Give me my shot!"

I then took the bike of her, but as I got on the bike and was ready to go my sister pushed me. I crashed into the pole. Well, you should have seen the sore face I had! I looked like a panda that had been in the wars. Two black eyes, bruises, scratches and scrapes all over my face. Not only that, it was worse, as my uncle (my dad's brother) was getting married a few days later and we were all supposed to be going. My mum took me to the the doctor and he said,
" I think her nose is broken, you will have to take her to the hospital."

12.

Once again we went on the bus to the hospital and everyone was looking at me, and my mum as if my mum had beaten me up. In the hospital the nurse asked my mum what happened, and she told her,

"She was playing in the back with her wee sister on the bike and her wee sister pushed her…she went into a pole. When I took her to the doctor he said he thinks her nose is broken."

I was given an x-ray but it wasn't broken, it was just 'badly swollen'. The nurse said to my mum,

"She'll be bruised but she's lucky that her glasses didn't break."

I'm not sure I'd have described the situation as lucky but there you go, the adults seemed to know what they were talking about!

I had to go to my Uncle's wedding like the war torn panda and everyone was looking and asking what happened. I felt a bit left out as I didn't want to run about too much incase I fell, so I just sat quietly with my mum and dad, beside my brothers and sisters and my Aunts, Uncles and cousins. I went into school the following Monday and when my friends came on the bus they were a bit stunned to see me. Astonished, almost all of them asked, one at a time,

"What happened to you?"

I told them what happened but they didn't believe me. They just said,

'That's rubbish!

Sister Mary also asked me the same,

"Margaret what happened to you?"

Yip, I had to go all over it again.

Home life with my mum, dad, brothers and sisters was good. It was a safe place to be. Of course we had ups and downs and *the odd arguments,* and I would get into a row from my mum because my sisters would tell my mum that I was cheeky and not doing what I was told, and that would always make me feel worse. I would go into a bad mood more as my wee sister seemed to get away with a lot. When something went wrong she would always say it wasn't her, and that it was me. But if we didn't do our chores, like washing the dishes and drying them we didn't get out to play. We had to keep our room tidy, and it was hard because there were four of us in the one room. My two older sisters were working so the younger two had to keep it tidy but it didn't always work out that way. When my two older sisters came in from work they used to just put all their stuff on the bed and it immediately made the room look untidy again. My brothers did their own room, or at least they were supposed to. I would help my mum make the dinner and if she needed anything from the shops, like bread and milk I would go for it. I really liked helping my mum and when my dad made the meatballs we would have pasta for dinner. They were amazing! When my dad was off on a Sunday he sometimes made gnocchi or minestrone soup. I remember my dad would have *Mario Lanza* on the record player and he would have all the windows open and the music up really loud. When this happened all the neighbours up the close would know that my dad was off work. They would say to my mum,

"Is Tony off today?"

My mum would just smile and say "aye", but she loved listening to Mario Lanza as well. My mum would sometimes make homemade dumpling and she would put it in an old pillow case and cook it for a couple of hours. Oh my goodness it was delicious! It was just so good.

Chapter 2

Lost

Going to visit my Auntie Margaret sometimes on a Tuesday my mum would take my wee sister and I to see my her as well. It was always on a Tuesday because that was the only day off my Auntie got as she worked in a toy shop in Clarkston. My dad was a twin and my Uncle Robert was married to my Auntie Margaret, so off we went to visit her. My sister and I would play down in the back garden or we would sit in the verandah with the cat. On one particular visit my mum and my aunt gave us money to go to the shop for sweets. The shop wasn't far, just along the road, but when we got there it was closed. So, Plan B: naturally, the quest for sweets continued and I said,

"We'll walk along to the other shop."

My two cousins said,

"No, we're not allowed."

Plan C: the quest must go on! I then said to my sister,

"We'll go and get the sweets."

We went, but as we were walking along the road I couldn't see the other shop and we ended up getting lost. I was only eight years old but there were two policemen walking towards us and they asked,

"Where are you going?"

I replied, "We were going for sweets but I think we've got lost."

They then asked, "Where do you stay?"

I said, quite casually, " Easterhouse."

Astonished, they asked, "What are you doing away down here?

15.

I said,
"We're visiting my auntie, my Auntie stayed over in the south-side."

Then they said, "Whereabouts in Easterhouse do you stay?"

I was eight years old so I could tell them almost everything. They took my sister and I to the police station and by this time my wee sister was crying. We were in the police station and they sat both of us on this big chair, my sister still crying, but I was ok. They gave us a piece of bread with jam and some milk to drink. Okay, it wasn't the sweets we had set out to get but I was happy because I was eating! Then the policeman asked if my auntie had a phone, and I said "yes". He then asked for the number, and they phoned to let my mum know that we were in the police station. My mum, my auntie and my two cousins came to get us as my mum didn't know where the police station was, when my mum came to get us she gave me into a row and told us we shouldn't have went any further when we saw that the shop was closed. But they only told us that after the event when we had already begun our search and were now lost, and found! My mum just took us home when we came out of the police station, we said cheerio to my auntie. My cousins said cheerio and that they would see us the following Tuesday. My mum and auntie took turns to visit and then it was my auntie's turn to come to our house. Such was the routine that my mum and my auntie did each week, and we went along with whatever they did. But after this I think they kept a closer eye on us and made sure that we knew not to wander off. I seemed to be developing a habit of going where I wasn't supposed to go or when I wasn't supposed to go.

When my two older sisters came home from work my mum told them what happened at my Auntie Margaret's. She told them not say anything to my dad when he came home from work. So when my dad came in from work we all had our dinner as normal and my dad was asking my mum,

" How are Robert and Sybil?"
My auntie Margaret's middle name was Sybil so that's what my mum and dad would call her. My mum was telling my dad that they were fine and the boys were good, but as my mum was speaking, my older sister Alice kept on laughing. My dad said,

"What are you laughing at?"

My sister said,

16.

"Margaret and Berta got lost when they were at my auntie Margarets the day, and they ended up in the police station."

Well, needless to say, my Dad went off his head, and he said to my mum,

"How did they get lost? Where you and Sybil too busy talking and not looking after them?"
My mum started to get upset because my dad was was shouting, and then I got upset. If my sister didn't just laugh all the time, it would have been ok, the coast would have been clear. But, as you might have guessed, I then got another telling of from my dad for doing what I did. I get that, but the thing is my sister was still laughing. She wanted us to get caught I think. Anyway, when I went into school on Monday I was telling my pals what had happened when I was at my Auntie's. I told them that my wee sister and I were in the police station, and as if we were real criminals they asked with deep curiosity,

"What was it like in the polis station?"

After we told them they just started to laugh and when I said,

" I've to get kept in when I go home from school… for a week!"

My pals sympathised, and understood the relentless quest for sugar and said,

"That's rubbish! You have to stay in for a week!"
I accepted my punishment humbly and admitted,

"Well, I did get us lost."

Chapter 3

Normal

I felt mixed.emotions at the thought of my pals out playing and me in the house. My pals who went to *the normal school* used to see me coming off the school bus and they saw some other kids calling me names so they ran up to them and told them to stop it and if they didn't stop it they would,

"Get a doing!"

But I said,

"No, don't fight."

But they were angry and said,

"They're calling you names and it's not nice."

I said, " I know, but my mum is coming to get me. "

This was all because I would go on the school bus and other boys and girls thought I was daft. Nevertheless, despite the cruel name calling I really enjoyed being at my primary and although I did go through some tests for me to go back to the normal school, I wasn't too bothered to go. When I was about 11 years old I was getting ready to go to my secondary school which was also *a special school* called, St Aidan's. It was in Bridgeton near where my big sister worked. Once again, my head teacher gave me a letter to give to my mum to say that they would like to speak to my mum and dad. My mum.came to the school even though my dad was working. I sat outside the Headteacher's office while Sister Mary spoke to my mum. It was also to say to my mum that the different tests I was getting were some of the subjects that the children get in the normal school and it was to see if I would be able to understand it and see how I got on with doing the tests. So, even though I passed everything, my mum said,

"This is a big change and there's different subjects in the normal school, and going to different classes for them, whereas Margaret is used to staying in the one class and all the subjects get done in the same class."

My mum continued,
" I'll speak to her dad tonight when he comes home form work."
When my dad came home from work we had our dinner and my dad asked my mum,

"What did the school want to see us about?"

My mum told him about the different test that I was getting in the school to see if I understood some of the different subjects that the children get in the normal school. But my dad said to me,

" How did you get on?"

My mum said,

" She passed everything, but if she goes to the normal school and goes into all the different classes for all the other subjects, and she isn't used to going into different classes, there could be a chance that she could fall behind. With a lot more going on now, and with it being her secondary school there could be a chance she might not fit in. And what if they start calling her names, especially if they ask what school did you come from?"

My mum and dad weren't happy at this and they asked me,

" How do you feel at going back to the normal school?

I said, "I don't want to go because if I get stuck at what to do with one of the subjects they will laugh at me and call me names… and if they found out the school I came from then they'll call me names. I want to stay at St Kenneth's and then go to St Aidan's."

So my dad simply said, "We aren't putting her through that again."

My mum then took me to school the next day to speak to the headteacher and Sister Mary, and to tell them that they wanted me to continue my time at St.Kenneth's and then go on to St Aidan's Secondary. I felt really happy that I was staying where I was and to be with my friends. I think it would have been very challenging and difficult if I wouldn't have fitted in. Meeting new people was difficult because I was so shy and I wouldn't speak up for myself. This was true even when I would go to Mass each week despite the fact that it played a big part in my life and it still does.

Sister Marie started up a playgroup and Sister Agnes took the younger children for liturgy each week. I would help out with tidying up when the Liturgy finished. Sister Marie also played the Guitar along with singing the hymns. I really enjoyed going to the after school club when I came home from school. I can remember this one time we were all about to play a game of rounders and Sister Marie announced,

"Just before we start, would any of you like to learn how to play the Guitar?
I said, " Yes, I would."

A couple of the other kids said yes as well. Sister Marie arranged the guitar lessons to be on a Wednesday after school, at 4-00 pm till 6-00pm. It was brilliant to learn how to play the guitar. I had a starter size for beginners and after a few months I got my own acoustic; the sound of it it was just amazing! After this, Sister Marie got a wee choir together to play at mass on the Sunday. I helped out at the church with different things that were going on with the after school club, and learning how to play the guitar. I just felt so good and happy because I was at the church. Even though I felt safe in my home surroundings the church community was special as well. I guess the important people in my life are my family and my friends but also at the Church Sister Marie, Sister Agnes, Father Jim and Father Michael were special to me. They brought a lot to the Church with what they had planned to do for Easterhouse.

As it was a *deprived area* they would have special prayer nights where they would be in the church and for the families to come and say special prayers. They would also organise 'Fun Days' for the younger children who were just starting school. When you're at the age of seven the boys and girls would be getting prepared to make their First Holy Communion and for the girls we would buy a *first holy communion* dress. It was all white, with a veil, gloves and I also had a red cape. I can remember that it was a really cold day and I was freezing. My mum had a heavy coat on and her head scarf. We got pictures took and we went into the school hall for breakfast, the Church had all of this organised, The boys wore suit trousers, a jacket and a shirt and tie. They would also come into the school for breakfast with their mum and dads. It was Father Jim who did the Mass and Sister Marie who helped with the service to make sure all the children were coming out to go to the altar. Father Jim would ask us to read our wee prayer that we had; the headteacher and all the teachers were also at the service, and sitting beside all the children who were making the first holy communion. It was a beautiful and special day even though it was a very cold day. When the service was finished my mum, dad and all my brothers and sisters went home, because in the sixties we didn't have the money to hire a lovely car or to hire a hall. Now we are in the 21st century its a big Event: sometimes the money spent might be taking away from what a special day making your first holy communion is all about. It's nice to see what the other children do for their first holy communion.

The feeling that you had when you walked into the Church was a warm welcoming, friendly feeling; this was your friends that you hadn't seen for a week and a chance to see them all there and have a good catch up. It was just an amazing feeling, and what the Sisters and Priests had planned to do for Easterhouse was just what we needed in the area. We didn't have anything or anywhere to go, and no matter what any of the parents were asked to do they said "no problem". They would do anything to help and organise anything that was planned for a fun day for the kids or a dance for the parents. They even gathered all our friends to raise funds to get other things for the children to play with, like new games, toys. They planned a day out to the zoo, at Heads of Ayr where they had horses, meerkats and rabbits; they even had a soft play area for the younger children. It was just amazing and everyone had a great day.
We would give all the children a packed lunch, with sandwiches, crisps and juice. There was a coach for the transport put on to take everyone away for the day and bring everyone back home. The pickup point and drop off was at St Claires Church.

When I went into school on Mondays, we were usually asked to write about what we did at the weekend, about when we went to mass and what else we did at the weekend. It was like a newsletter we were to do each week, every Monday.
And then we would do our reading, sums and say all the times-table together. Sister Bernadette would ask some of us to collect go round and collect our sum jotters for her to look at them to correct, and when she was finished she would call your name and you would go to her desk. Then she would go over any of your sums that you got wrong (if any), but you couldn't tell if anyone got any of them wrong as she was gentle and kind and sensitive to your spirit.

St Aidan's school was great, a beautiful set of memories for me. Sister Bernadette and all the other teachers were brilliant, so lovely. They were always so kind and had time to talk to you if you were not sure of anything about at all. To have this loving

21.

attention is priceless. I could see and feel then that this was what I, and so many others really needed, some loving attention by kind souls to nurture our sensitive hearts.

Chapter 4

Grief

When I was twelve years old I experienced grief for the very first time. My uncle Guy (my dad's brother) was killed in a horrific lorry crash on the motorway, he was a long-distance lorry driver, and he would deliver long steel beams to all different parts of the country.

When I got home from school my mum said that there was a very bad lorry crash on the motorway, and that my Auntie Nora (my uncle Guy's wife) had phoned my mum to get in contact with my dad at his work. It was my uncle Guy's lorry that crashed and it was really bad, the news came on at 6-00pm and it was on the news. They showed the crash, and it looked really terrible, my mum got in contact with my dad at his work and my dad went straight to the hospital. My auntie Nora and my cousins were at the hospital when my dad got there.

I will never forget, when my dad came home. My mum said,
"How is Guy?"

My dad just broke down and cried.

We had a radiogram and I saw my dad bend over it and crying. He said to my mum that Guy had died and that the crash was really bad. My dad said that steel beams Guy had on his lorry went straight through to the cabin and that there was no chance of saving him. It was so sad.

This was the first time I had ever saw my dad cry, everything just felt so different. We were all so upset and the hurt to see my dad feeling so sad. It was heart-breaking to see my dad and my mum crying and holding each other. What else could they do? What can anyone do at times like these? When I went into school the following Monday the headteacher and Sister Bernadette called me out of the classroom to ask if it was my uncle that had been killed in the lorry crash. I said,
"Yes, he was my dad's brother"
They asked me If I was ok to be in school. Their kindness touched my heart and I got

upset. I said I was okay, but the headteacher sent me home anyway. She said she'd phone my mum to let her know that she was sending me home, and that they were sorry to hear about my uncle.

My Uncle Guy, my auntie Nora and my cousins were such good family. My uncle guy played in a band, and he played the accordion and sang, he was great. When he would play at the weekend my mum and dad would go and see him with my auntie Nora. He was a long-distance driver for many years, and he loved what he did and playing in the band.

My dad was one of four siblings; he had a twin brother, an older sister and a younger brother. My mum and dad helped my auntie Nora with the funeral arrangements for my uncle. What a sad day it was. I can remember there were lots of my uncle's friends, his band mates and even friends from the pubs where he used to play. My dad, mum and all of the family went to visit my auntie Nora every week. It just felt so strange when we went to visit my auntie not to see my uncle Guy there. It felt as if he was just away out, but as the weeks went on then I began to realise that we weren't going to see him again. Grief is difficult to come to terms with.That was the very first time I had ever experienced the loss of a family relation, and it was such a deep sadness to see my dad broken-hearted at losing his brother.

When I went back to school after a couple of days off, my headteacher and Sr Bernadette asked me was I feeling okay. I said, "Yes, I'll be ok." My friends also asked me how I was. I said was ok, but it was strange to have experienced loss at this age. My friends were really great pals and we all got on so well, even when we went to the after school club that had started up. It was really good as we would listen to all different kinds of music and even some that I listened to when my mum and dad would have a wee family get-together. It just made me feel relaxed being with my friends, especially as it was an emotional time in our family. When we went to mass there were prayers said for all my family, including my auntie Nora and all my cousins as well. Everyone at mass paid their condolences to my mum and dad. Father Jim, Sister Marie and Sister Agnes were speaking to my mum and dad after mass had finished and then we all went into the tea room for tea, coffee and biscuits. To spend time with our friends, our family and those of our faith helped us to get through this difficult time. Everyone was so nice, so kind to us. The lovely warm compassion and sensitivity at mass made it feel like it really was your extended family. It was beautiful. A light in a dark time.

I would often meet my friends at chapel whom I sometimes wouldn't see from week to week. These were my friends when I started primary school at St Claires. We still remained pals even though I went to 'a special school'. They would say,

"It makes no difference we are all pals. "

We would talk about what kind of week we had in school and with me having all my subjects in the one class, they would often say, "I wish we stayed in the one class." They told me that they had to go to different classes for different subjects and they would need to go to three or four different classes a day. I said, "I couldn't be bothered with that." So, I was so glad that I stayed at St Aidan's until I was ready to leave school but I still had three years to go until I left. I kept playing the guitar and singing in the choir at mass because I felt happy doing this. It was a great feeling inside and the sound of the acoustic guitar was just an amazing sound. The music and my faith, my community and my family were all a growing part of a little light within me.

Chapter 5

My Special Place
(Schoenstatt Shrine)

When Sister Marie, Sister Agnes and Father Jim went on their sabbaticals, they would go to Schoenstatt Shrine, Sisters of Mary.

Schoenstatt Scotland is a Religious Retreat and Pilgrimage Centre, and when Sister Marie came back from her sabbatical, I asked Sister Marie all about Schoenstatt and whether it opened to the public. Sister Marie said, "Yes of course it is." So, I asked Sister Marie how I would get there on the bus. I found out I could get the X19 from Easterhouse into the city centre and get off at the Glasgow royal infirmary, cross the road to the bus stop that the X85 stops at, and then get that straight into Campsie Glen. From the bus terminus in Campsie Glen and it was only a five minute walk. I was told to go in the back way to the grounds and when I got there, "Wow!" It is so beautiful. That's the way I go in all the time now, because there is a water lake that you pass, and the sound of running water. Well, it just makes me feel so relaxed and it's so peaceful. I didn't know it was open to the public to walk around, but Sister Marie said, "Nowadays it's open to all."

It has the smallest church in Scotland and you can see the stone stations of the Cross. Up on the hill of the grounds you can see the Schoenstatt Shrine. I just love going to Schoenstatt every couple of weeks. If the weather hasn't been so good, which is highly likely as it is Scotland, then I'd try to go at least once a month. I do like to go as often as I can, especially with it being open all year round. There are many walks around the estate and the attractions it has around the grounds are so stunning. There is also a café with fresh bean coffee; I prefer tea though but there is a wide selection of drinks and food as well.

It is also a lovely journey on the bus going out to Schoenstatt. Traveling by bus and watching the scenery as you go happily by is just so beautiful. I absolutely love going to my special place, and every time I go without fail I feel so relaxed. It clears my mind to get away for a few hours. I sometimes feel as if I'm in another country, and I always see something different each time I go. I spend a few hours there and I stay for the afternoon mass, and it's always a beautiful service. The simple things in life are sometimes the most precious and beautiful.

Schoenstatt Sisters Of Mary
Scotland

Sisters Margareta & Mary Elsbeth are from the community of the Schoenstatt Sisters of Mary which was founded in Germany on October 1, 1926, by Father Joseph Kentenich. The Sisters are one of six Secular Institutes belonging to the Schoenstatt Family. They are a community of consecrated woman who have committed themselves to surrender to God in the Spirit of the Evangelical Counsels. They possess a marked secular character; that is, they live their ideal of surrender to God amidst the world. At the present time there are three sisters at Schoenstatt Scotland, Below the Schoenstatt Sisters of Mary Scotland.

Schoenstatt is a Catholic lay Marian movement which strives to live the Gospel of Jesus Christ through the example and guidance of Mary, the mother of God. Schoenstatt was founded on October 18, 1914, by Fr Joseph Kentenich in the little Schoenstatt valley in the Rhine region of west-central Germany.

Chapter 6

The Ibrox Disaster, 1971

When I was about thirteen years old, my dad and my older brother went to all the football matches as they were, like most Catholics in Glasgow, Celtic Supporters. They went to every game on a Saturday, usually. So, on one particular Saturday in 1971 it was an 'old firm' game, between Celtic and their city rivals, Rangers. Around the ninetieth minute, Celtic took a 1-0 lead through a Jimmy Johnstone goal, but in the final moments of the match, Colin Stein scored an equaliser for Rangers. As thousands of spectators were leaving the ground by stairway 13, it was reported that it appeared someone may have fallen, causing a massive chain-reaction pile-up of devoted fans. As they began to try to exit the stadium at the blow of the final whistle, one or two people accidentally slipped. Stairway 13 was packed with supporters, as it often was, and as waves of people gained momentum, they could not see that others had fallen. A terrible crush ensued. It was tragic.

Most of the deaths that occurred are recorded as being caused by 'compressive asphyxia'. Everyone who died was under fifty years of age, and many of the injured fans received life-saving treatment whilst laying on the stairways. My dad and my older brother were also at the old firm game, but they left well before Celtic scored the first because up until that time no one had scored. So, when a news flash came on the television about what had happened at the football, and my mum, my sisters and my other brothers heard this we were all upset and worried at what happened. We hadn't heard anything from my dad and my brother, because we didn't have any mobile phones in the early 70s. So, my dad and my brother had gone to the pub because of the way the game was going and with no score near the end. Our next door neighbour, Mrs Marshall, chapped our door and asked my mum, if Tony (my dad) and my brother, who is also called Tony, were home from the football. She knew they always went to the football, and she heard what had happened at Ibrox. My mum said that they weren't home yet and they hadn't phoned. We were all in a state of worry with no message from them. However, about 10-30 p.m. my dad and brother came home, and my mum anxious and irritated said to them,

"What kept you?"

My dad said, "We left the game early because they hadn't scored and it was getting too near the end of the game.",

My mum was so angry at my dad and my brother, but we all just cried and were relieved that they came home. My dad, oblivious to what had taken place said, "How, what's happened?"

My mum said, "There's been a really bad disaster at Ibrox. When some of the fans were leaving early, they thought they heard someone score, but a couple of them slipped and there were so many fans leaving that they didn't see how bad it was in front of them."

My dad and brother couldn't believe what my mum was telling them. Just about then another news flash came on the television. My dad and my brother were shocked, they couldn't believe what happened and they got quite upset at the thought of what could have happened. They realised now why my mum was so angry with them. But what a relief! Thank God they had left early and were safe. Our next-door neighbour, Mrs Marshall chapped the door to see if my dad and my brother were home yet and to see if they were okay. My mum said, "Yes, they're not long home…they left the game early because there was no score, and it was coming to near the end of the game."

Mrs Marshall said to my mum, " Well, that's good that they're home safe." They spoke about what had happened and how sad it was. It was a tragedy for the whole city, many families were devastated by it.

To this day, on the 2nd January the date of the Ibrox Disaster, there is a memorial service and every football game that's played in Glasgow on this day hold a two-minute silence. All the football players wear black bands to commemorate all the people who died on that day. And to this day, it is the worst football stadium disaster in Scotland and the ninth worst in the world. Ibrox was largely rebuilt and renewed after this. The vast bowl-shaped terracing was removed and replaced by three rectangular all-seated stands by 1981. After renovations were completed in 1997, the ground was renamed Ibrox Stadium.

Reconstruction began in August 1978.

Chapter 7

Teenage Years

When I went back into school the following Monday my pals and I were talking about what had happened at the football at Ibrox. My pals also had their dads and most of them had brothers at the old firm match, but they were all ok. We all just felt so relieved that they got home safe. There was a deep sadness about everything that had happened so the atmosphere in school felt so strange. When we got into the classroom, we usually stood to say our prayers first, but Sister Bernadette said, "Before we start our prayers, did you all see the news at the weekend ? And about what happened at the old firm football game at Ibrox on Saturday?"
We all said, " Yes Sister",
Then Sister Bernadette said, "As we say our prayers we will pray for all the people that died, and all their families and everyone who was injured and all their families. We will give thanks for all of us who had family at the football who came home safe. Before we start we will do a one minute silence. And to-day we will all be going to St Mary's for a special Mass at 11-00 am. Father Michael will be saying mass and as we go into the Church, we will all receive a candle to light before Mass starts and it will stay lit until we do a one-minute silence."
The feeling I had was sad, it was painful; to think of all those people who died or were injured, and their poor families. After Mass we all went back to school, in class Sister Bernadette said, "The school is going to fundraise to help with the Ibrox Park Disaster Fund and is also going to arrange a school fete to raise funds. It will be held in the school dining hall. There will be lots of parents helping on the day."

We had flyers made out to advertise the fete with all the information on it as, what time and day it would be on and what we had on the tables to sell. We had home baking, toys, games, arts and crafts and homemade tablet and truffles.

It was an amazing day at the fete, the school raised. 500 pounds for the Ibrox Park Disaster Fund. There were a lot of different events taking place to fundraise: A one-off club tournament, the British League Cup, while Rangers' old Firm rivals Celtic organised a match against English side Blackburn Rovers to raise funds. An Ibrox Park disaster fund was established in aid of the victims and ran for nearly two years before being disbanded.

The Stairway is gone but the memories remain. The events of that cold January day remain clear in the mind. Donald S Taylor is the co-author, along with Paul Collier, of "Stairway 13- The Story of the 1971 Ibrox Disaster" (published by Bluecoat Press). It is a day that some Glaswegians, and hopefully all, will never forget as it was deeply tragic, but the response also showed the love and unity of the people of the city. Despite the usual fierce rivalry between Celtic and Rangers, with its religious associations and long history, a horrific event showed that there was real human love and compassion, a true willingness to help and be there for each other. Another beautiful light in a sometimes dark city.

Chapter 8

Moving on

Just before I was 'getting organised' to leave my Secondary School and to find a job, we had a Career's Officer who came into the school to speak to us about what kind of work we were interested in. We all spoke about different things. So, when I used to go on the 'corpy' bus (Glasgow Bus Corporation) we had a bus conductor who would come round all the passengers and ask, "Where are you going?" so that he would give you the right bus ticket, and I had thought at one point, "I really like the wee ticket machine so I think I want to be a bus Conductress." simply because I liked the ticket machine, but thankfully the thought of that didn't last too long. I had a big brother and sister who worked in the Canda at Queenslie Industrial Estate, so, they said that they would get me a job where they worked because there were job vacancies and they were looking for more people. When the careers officer came into the school to see me, his name was Mr Murray and after a brief chat he asked me what kind of job I'd be interested in. I said to him at first,

"I was thinking about being a bus conductress because I really liked the ticket machine that they use." He just smiled and said, "What kind of other jobs did you have in mind?" I then told him that I had a big brother and sister who work in the Canda. My brother worked in the cutting, cutting all the material for the garments and coats that were made. My big sister was a machinist, making skirts, trousers and doing repairs if any of the garments came back from quality control. They were looking for more people, so I said to Mr Murray that I'd like to apply for a job there. So, he said, "I can help you to do that and to apply for anything else that I can think of. So, I applied for the job for the Canda, and I got it! I would start as soon as I left school. A couple of my friends did the same and applied for a job there as well, because I'd said to them that they were looking for more people to start. They also got a job to start the same time when we would all be leaving school.

I had a great time at my secondary school and being with my friends we would have a good time, more so when we went to the after school club which was still in the school. It would start when school finished at 3-30pm and it would be on until 5-30pm. We would listen to all different types of vinyl records, that we all liked. We had an old fashioned record player, though it was a new one then, and we would also have one of the teachers there to make sure there wasn't any trouble. On one occasion a couple of the boys started an argument but before it went any further, the teacher stepped in to stop them; things could get rough in Easterhouse if left unchecked. They were barred from coming to the club for two weeks, but they were told when they came back to the club if they started anything again they'd not be allowed back.

So, when they did come back there was no more trouble. I think a wee break made them realise what they were missing out on. I really liked my music and listening to the top-twenty every Sunday on the radio. I used to record it but trying to cut out the adverts was a nightmare! I'd be listening for the end of the song to finish and to get ready to pause the tape so I could miss the adverts out.

In my teenage days when I was just about to leave secondary school, we had a Mass for all the ones that were leaving. When the mass was finished, we had a gathering in the school dining hall, where we had sandwiches, cakes, soft drinks, tea and coffee. I left school when I was sixteen years old, this was in the early 1980s. We didn't have any proms in that time like they have now.

The most we got was a gathering in the school hall where Father Michael and the headteacher would say a speech to wish all the school leavers well in their jobs, that they were going to start on the following Monday. Not long after the speeches we all started to leave. That was that. No drama, no excitement, but just a bit of anticipation about entering into the world of work and adult responsibilities.

Chapter 9

Starting Work

The day before I started work was a Sunday night. I was a bag of nerves. I felt sick, nor could I sleep. My mum said, "You'll be fine, because John and Marie will be going to work with you. My brother could drive so he could take my big sister and I to work and we would all finish at the same time as well.
When I went in to the building my sister said, "Wait here."
I said, "What for?"
"The supervisor will come along and show you round the factory, where the fire points are and the canteen and stuff."
She advised me and it was good to have her there. So, the supervisor came, her name was Janet and she showed me all around the factory: where the cutting room was, the canteen, the stock room and what to do and where to go if there was a fire. She then took me to meet the girl who was the 'button machinist', her name was Mary, and I was told that she would be showing me what to do and how to put the buttons on all different kinds of materials on the coats. This was due to the fact that the machine would have to be set for thick buttons, and then it would have to be changed for the thinner buttons for the lighter coats.
So, she was showing me what to do, it was two button machines side by side, and it was like a wee bench we sat; she would do one side, and she showed me how to put the buttons on the other side. I would do one side and Mary would do the first side on the left of the coat, and then she would pass it over to me to do the right side because they were double breasted coats that we were doing for the winter. We would do different kinds of coats, light ones as well. And the colours were amazing, beautiful.

I still felt nerves for a few weeks, but then I started to get used to it and I started to like it a bit more. But I wasn't even working there for a year in the job, and we were all made redundant, I was really upset, more so as it was my first job.
So, I had to go to 'the broo', the unemployment office in Glasgow where you signed on for support. That's what we did in the early seventies if you lost your job.
That's what it was called in those days, and they would help you try and find another job like the type of job that you were doing, I did find another job myself, and it was

another job for a button machinist.

The name of the factory was called 'Collins Ltd'; they were based at Royston Road in Glasgow. I had to get the bus too, and it left me off at the main road, and then I would have about a five minute walk. The bus was a number 211, it was the old Eastern Scottish buses and at that time they had no doors on them, they were called 'the back-ender buses'. My time in 'Collins' was pretty good. It wasn't really a big factory, well not as big as the Canda, but everyone I worked with were nice and friendly. It was a positive, happy atmosphere. I was only about two years working for them and 'it happened' again, redundancy. But this time the factory went into liquidation and the re-services came in to close the factory down. So, I had to go to 'the broo' again, to explain what had happened where I worked.

At this point I said to my mum and dad, that I wasn't going back into machining because I thought I was a 'bit of a Jinx', which means bad luck. My mum and dad said in a synchronised voice, "What are you going to do?"

I said, "I'll go to the broo and see what they have got."

Back to 'the broo' I went, and I saw that they had vacancies for Lewis's, the big store in Glasgow City Centre on Argyle St. Lewis's was the landmark of the biggest stores in Glasgow. So, I asked at the desk in 'the broo' about the vacancies that Lewis was advertising, and the man I spoke to said it was for kitchen assistants, to help with food preparation and to help cook the food.

I said, "That sounds good, can I apply for it?"

He said, "Just phone this number, speak to the personnel, it will be them that will answer the phone. They will ask you a few questions and then arrange for you to come for an interview."

So, I phoned. They just asked my name and how old I was, and then they said, "Can you come for an interview?"

I excitedly replied, "Yes, of course!"

I went for the interview and they asked a few more questions about where I worked before and why I left. I told them, "I didn't leave the first job as I was made redundant from it as it closed down; the second job I had the company went into liquidation… so after that I thought maybe being a machinist wasn't for me. I wanted to try something different."

35.

After the interview finished they told me that I had the job and to start the following Monday.
I was delighted. I said, "Thank-you I'm looking forward to it." And I was!

Wow! I felt so excited and couldn't wait to get home to tell my mum and dad, they were happy and said, "That's great, you'll enjoy that." Helping my mum in the house with the cooking as a child gave me some idea of what I would be doing.
When I started in Lewis's, the head chef was called Stewart, and he showed me around the kitchen and introduced me to all the staff, and then he explained everything that we had to do in the kitchen. I was working in the Cafeteria on the fifth floor, and the chef said, "On every Wednesday morning at 9-00 am there is a fire drill, so every department has their own coded colour to let them know when to go. So, when the lights flash then that's your department and everyone can make their way to the furthest away fire door to exit the building. We have a colour chart as well and everyone looks at it to see what department it was. That will tell you whatever light colour flashed on the day of the fire drill, that would be in that department."

I was working along with Liz and Lisa, and they were very helpful and showed me what to do, and that the time of service starts at 10-00am. It was waitress service so whatever the customer orders the waitress came in with an order we just served everything up and put it on the hot serving counter, and they took it and served the customer. I really enjoyed my first day and there was so much to do. I couldn't wait to tell my mum and dad how my day went when I got home. So, this was the beginning of my catering experience and my career starting off.
I worked in Lewis's for just over nine years when we heard talks about the store possibly being put up for sale. All the staff couldn't believe it, or didn't want to, but it was true. We heard that Debenhams was taking it over and that we had to re-apply for our jobs and the position that we currently had, or you could take your redundancy. I took my redundancy and decided to move on.

Chapter 10
Moving on...again!

I decided to move on and in those days you could get a catering job quite easily. It wasn't long until I got another job as a commis chef in The Rotunda. The Rotunda was a well known restaurant beside where the Scottish Exhibition Centre is now, down by the Clyde-side. There were two of the same buildings built for 'The Garden Festival', which was the biggest event in Scotland since the Empire Exhibition fifty years earlier. It ran between April and September 1988, and it took place on a 120-acre site around the former Prince's Dock, on the south bank of the river Clyde. That's where the second Rotunda building was. The Glasgow Harbour Tunnel Rotundas are two red brick stone Rotundas which flank the river Clyde in Glasgow, Scotland. The North Rotunda is located on Tunnel Street in the Finnieston area of Glasgow, with the South Rotunda at Plantation Place in Govan.

On my first day as a Commis Chef the Head Chef introduced me to the second Chef and all the other Chefs that you would assist a section Chef, also known as a 'Chef De Partie'. The Head Chef also showed me round the Bistro on the ground floor as you enter the building beside the reception area. On the second floor, where the Italian Restaurant was, was where I was going to be working. On the second floor was the French Restaurant and Richard was the head Chef of the restaurant, and he introduced me to the other Chefs.

The role was made up of varying responsibilities including: assisting in the food preparation process; cooking and preparing elements of high-quality dishes; preparing meats, chicken, fish and vegetables. A commis is a junior member of staff who works under a 'chef de parties' to learn the ins and outs of a specific station. These are often people who have recently completed or are still undertaking formal culinary training such as an apprenticeship and are gaining real-world experience. I was around nineteen years old when I started in the Rotunda. It was an Italian Restaurant and it was very suitable with me being part Italian (my dad's Mum and Dad were Italian). My grandparents had came over from Italy in their early teens, but I'll tell you more about my family later.

37.

When I started, the head chef introduced me to the second chef, we had a pastry chef and all the 'chef de parties'. I was the only girl in the kitchen, I say 'girl', I was in my late teens. I was a few hours into my shift and Brian who I was working along with said to me, "Can you go up and ask Richard for a long stand?" I complied. Now at this point I didn't know that this is what they do to all new chefs (to play a joke) so I went up and said to Richard, "Have you got a long stand?" He just laughed, I said, "Have I asked for the wrong thing'?
Richard said, "No it's a joke that they like to do when new Chefs start."
I got it and said, "Oh, ha-ha!" I went back down to the kitchen and the Chefs were all laughing; talk about having a red face! It was funny, but I was really embarrassed. I suppose this is just the way of new starts and job patter.

I got on with what I was showed to do, and it was amazing learning all these starters, that were on the menu. I got showed how to clean and gut fish, cut raw meat, like chicken, etc. Learning all this was amazing, and working as a commis chef for a good few months, I picked up the ins and outs very quick, and then I was made up to a 'chef de partie'. Having more responsibility, I worked on the starter section and when a check came on for starters, mains or desserts the head chef would call everything out and all the chefs had to answer and acknowledge that you heard what the chef called out, and you would reply, "Yes chef!"

After I worked on the starters and got to know everything about the section I got put on to the pizza section and got showed how to make the dough for the pizzas and to make the bread also. I really loved it and enjoyed it so much. I would then get put on to all the other sections to learn them and then once I learned all the ins and outs of each section, the chef would do the rota and you would get put on to any section each week. All this would also include going down to the basement to the walk-in fridge. Wow! I had never seen a walk-in-fridge this size before, where all the back-up food was kept to keep it fresh, and we would just take whatever we would need. I was about three years in and the second Chef left so the head Chef spoke to the owners to offer me the second chef position. But with the owners' being Italian I had to prove myself all the time because I was the first women that they ever had working in their kitchen. I felt as if I had to let them see that I was more than capable of doing the job. The owners said no to the Chef and that they would look for a second Chef.

The head Chef was so annoyed when he came back into the kitchen. He spoke to me to let me know what they said, I said to the chef it was ok, but I will get the position, one of these days. A second chef started and he lasted three months. So, again the head chef spoke to the owners and again they said the same thing. This happened on three occasions and then the chef said to the owners that I was more than capable of doing the job as second Chef. Finally, they gave me a chance and said to the Chef that it would be a months trial. When the chef came back into the kitchen he said, "They are giving you a months trial."
I said to the head chef "That's good! It's time to prove them wrong."
 Yippee! I sure did prove them wrong. After my trial was up the owners asked for the Chef and myself to come and speak to them.
After we spoke, they said that they were pleased at the job I was doing, and they offered me the job as second Chef.
Oh, wow! I felt so pleased with myself and proud of what I had done to get this far. I was working in the Rotunda for nearly ten years, and then the bad news came that the owners were selling up. The sad that whoever buys it must do so on the condition that they keep all the Chefs and staff. So, the owners from the company, Leonardo's Ltd came in to look round and then they came back a second time to meet all the chefs and staff. They became our new owners.

The new owners had other restaurants, in Dundee, Ireland and Aberdeen, and they were not long opened. They were looking to open another restaurant in London, but they went into liquidation because each restaurant didn't have enough time to get off the ground and make their mark, so the receivers came in and closed all the restaurants down. All the staff that worked for them lost all their money that was owed to them and holiday pay also. So, back to the drawing board I went, looking for another job..again! I still wanted to stay in catering and get another chef's job.
And that is what I did! I got another chef's job in Sarti's, an Italian restaurant in the city centre at the top of Hope Street. Again, it was a great job. The owners were amazing to work with and all good chefs. They had a smaller restaurant upstairs

facing onto Waterloo Street, and sometimes each of us would be sent up to that one to work in also. The Chef would do a rota for each of us to take a turn on a weekly basis.

The restaurants were amazing to work in, and very busy, but it was long hours and split shifts. Sometimes I would start at 9 am until 2-30 pm. I'd have a two hour break and then I'd be back for 5pm for the evening shift. We would do a pre-theatre menu because we were beside The Glasgow Royal Concert Hall, where a lot of concerts were held. I went to a few on my days off, providing it was a concert that I would go to.

When there were concerts it was a very busy time. We would take a break for an hour if we were lucky. I was on the pizza section and had to make sure that we were well prepped up for it getting busy. We were working nonstop to make sure we had plenty of pizzas rolled out and plenty of bread made. We could do up to about two hundred covers a night when concerts or any other events were on. It was definitely a very busy area and beside Sarti's there was the Theatre Halls, not far from the restaurant. We would all finish about 11pm at night but by the time we all cleared up it would be nearer 12-00pm. when we would finish. By the time I got home I had to unwind, so I would have a shower and a wee cuppa. It would be after 1-00 am before I would get to bed, and then back up at 7-00am to get organised and do it all again!

Yes, it was a very long day and long hours, but I enjoyed what I did. Receiving feedback from customers saying that they enjoyed their meal was always amazing. It made my day so worthwhile, and made me feel so good, at what I did. It was awesome.

Chapter 11

The Family Home

My dad was a real family man with strong roots in his own family and the traditions of his parents. They were Italians, and I know that my Granda was born in 1898, but I'm not sure when my Gran ('Nona' in Italian) was born. I do know that my Gran died before I was born in the late 50s. I was born in 1958 and my dad was one of ten siblings, but tragically there was a house fire and five of my dad's siblings died. There were also a set of twins, but I'm not sure how many brothers and sisters there were. My dad was also a twin, and was the oldest sibling, of two younger brothers and one sister; the five of them got saved as well as my Gran and Granda.

My dad's parents came over to Britain from Italy in their early teens, to have a better life. They opened a fish and chip shop in Tollcross in Glasgow, and it was known as 'the best fish and chip shop in the city'. The customers came from all over because they said it was the best fish and chips they had ever tasted.When I was a bit older my mum and dad used to tell us stories of what my Gran and Granda did. They stayed in the back shop of the fish and chip shop to start off with, before they finally got a house. My dad said that my Gran used to give my dad's younger brother John, a telling off in Italian because he wouldn't share his sweets with my dad and the rest of his siblings. We loved all the old stories and just laughed. My dad said it didn't make any difference because he still didn't share them. It was so funny. My gran and Granda were very hard working and worked very long hours to give my dad and his brothers and sister the best that they could.

When my dad left school he went straight into the army, and he said, that's just what happened in those days. When my dad was in the army he met my mum. She was a cook and they started seeing each other. My mum would always tell us that she didn't like the army. My mum's Mum had died when she was only four years old. My mum's dad (my Granda) was a lovely man. He was so kind. My mum would take us to see my Granda every week, but when my Granda met another woman, they got married when my mum was thirteen years. old. Things started to change a bit because she didn't like my mum, and my mum wasn't keen on her either. My mum used to say we were not to call her Gran, but we were to call her 'Auntie Lizzie'. My mum was one of three siblings. She had two older brothers and also had five step siblings: four sisters and one brother. They didn't get on very well, my mum was really close to her two brothers, Tony and Robert.

As I said earlier, my mum was in the army and she often told us that she didn't like it. She said that one time she was on leave and came home to her dad's house, but when it was time for her to go back to the army she didn't go. She went 'A-wall', as they called it in those days. The army sent the Military Police to come and find my mum and to arrest her for not going back to the army after her leave was finished, she was put in military jail but soon left the army. My mum and dad still stayed in touch, I can't remember the regiment they were in, but this was the one they later got married in, in
1948. My mum was only twenty-one years old, and my dad was twenty six.

They set up life in Duke Street in Glasgow. It was a one bed-sit with just a kitchen off the bedroom; it was an outside toilet and we had a tin bath. My dad got a job after he came out of the army, as a barber. He used to cut my hair and my brothers and sisters hair as well. We can laugh now but it wasn't that funny as it looked as if my dad put a bowl over our head and cut round it. But that's what had to happen in those days because then I was one of seven siblings. We stayed in Duke Street when my mum and dad got married and it was a few years we stayed there. Yes, times were hard when my mum and dad got married and started a family. My dad worked all the hours he could to give us as much as they could, and my mum would look after all of us because there were no nurseries or baby sitters in those days.

We sometimes had power cuts where we had no electricity, so we used to light candles to give us some light. It was a coal fire that we had and when we needed to get the coal for it to stay lit my mum or dad went out to the cellar for the coal which was kept in a bucket beside the fire. The telly that we had was an old black and white one and my mum and dad had to put fifty pence in it for it to work. It was the same for the gas and the electric; it was meters also. It was a time of poverty in those days and for a good few years but it didn't stop us from being happy with family.

42.

My mum and dad always gave us what they could and even when it was Christmas time, we would all hang up our socks (not Christmas stockings) in those day, and we would get a Tangerine, an apple and some chocolate.

I was born on Christmas day, so I got a wee bit more, and again it was what my mum and dad could afford, because it was just my dad that was working at this point even though my mum would get 'family allowance' as it was in those days. Things were still hard. My dad worked in the barbers until it ended up closing, but it wasn't long before he got another job. It was in Partick in a scrap yard. He worked there for years until he retired, but my dad stayed on working with 'Robinsons', and no matter what you were looking for my dad would always say,
"You will get that in Partick, it's a great place."
We would all laugh, and my dad said,
"What are you laughing at?"
My mum would say, "No matter what you're looking for you always say you will get that in Partick."
It became a family joke, as if Partick was some magical land where you could find anything. Even till this day we still say it and just have a smile, because it holds beautiful memories for us. I will always remember the time when my Granda came to stay with us, when he wasn't able to stay by himself any more. He would always wear his hat, even sometimes sitting on the chair. He would hold my younger brother, Mario, when he was just a baby. It was just so lovely to sit and watch.

I will always remember when we were growing up and moved to Easterhouse. My dad came home from work and one of his pals' dogs had pups, so my dad spoke to my mum to ask if I could get one of them. My mum said yes, but the siblings and I knew nothing at the time. When my dad came home from work, my younger sister and I were out playing and we saw him coming home, so we ran up to him and he was holding his works jacket closed. He had a big inside pocket in his jacket and he said, "I've got something in my jacket for you, come in to the house."
I said impatiently, "What is it?"
He said, " Just wait till we get in."
As soon as we got into the house my mum said to my dad, "Did you get it?'

My dad said "aye". I couldn't wait. I was bursting with excitement, again I said, "What is it?"
Then he showed us; it was a wee pup. He was so adorable and we called him Bruno he was all black. My dad said to all of us, "You will have to all take a turn and take him out. I'll show youse how to train him so that he'll still do the same for youse when I'm at work."
We trained him along with my dad. I just loved taking him out for walks and over to the field for a run about. When I came home from school and before I helped mum to get the dinner ready I took Bruno out for a walk, and then I helped mum get the dinner ready for my dad coming in from work and my older sisters and brothers were working at this point as well. I just loved having a dog, he was just so loving. We trained him to "give us a paw...wait at the curb to cross the road... and to walk beside you and not to run away." He was so obedient and did what he was told.
Then he would get a treat. Bruno was our first dog and first experience of growing up with a pet. Then I got a budgie, and I named him Joey, I taught him to talk, it was amazing he could say his name and, "Where's Joey?"

My mum and dad were amazing! They were so caring and loving and the stories they used to tell us when we were all small were great. I remember my mum telling us, when I was still a baby, that when we stayed in Duke Street, we had a cat and it used to sit at the window while the window was open. My older brother, Tony, would get the sweeping brush and the window was open just enough for the cat to sit on the windowsill, well Tony pushed the cat off the windowsill, and my mum said, "Where's the cat?"
Tony said, "I pushed it off the windowsill."
But the next thing the cat came back up to the door and my mum gave Tony a telling off and told him not to do that again. He never did it again because when my dad came home from work, my mum told him what Tony did, so he got another telling off.

I would often watch my mum and dad cooking the dinner: my dad made meatballs, and homemade Gnocchi, or we would have a different kind of pasta. He would also make Sugo, meaning 'sauce' in Italian, it's a traditional tomato base sauce. It was just amazing to watch and learn, and my mum would also make homemade dumpling. Wow! It was amazing, the best ever, and before I went into catering to be a Chef, I had two of the best teachers in my life: Mum and Dad. They showed me the ropes about how to cook and it all came together when I went into catering. When my older sisters and brother got married (Maria, Tony and Alice) well let's just say the weather wasn't that great, it is Glasgow of course. It was amazing! All my aunts, uncles, cousins and their friends came, and it was a great celebration and to catch up with everyone.

When my older brother John got married to Pat it was a double wedding, Pat's sister Susan and her husband Allan got married, what a brilliant day. I can remember the weather, it was a sunny day and what another great celebration it was with all the families from both sides and all our relatives and friends, it was just so lovely to meet so many people. And after a couple of years, at different times of course, they all started a family. It was so lovely to have nieces and nephews, and to be an Auntie.
When all the older sisters and brothers got married, it left mum, dad, me my younger sister Roberta and my younger brother Mario, and Bruno in the house. After a few years my younger sister Roberta got married to Robert, it was a lovely celebration to have all the aunts, uncles, cousins and all their friends there was another fantastic day.

So with five of my siblings married, and with it just being my mum, dad my younger brother Mario and myself, the house that we were in was a bit too big, so my mum and dad put in for another house, we then moved not far from were we stayed, it was only walking distance but it was a back and front door, and the house was amazing. It wasn't far from Mario's school, St Collette's primary school. We also stayed beside another primary school called 'Common Head". Some of Mario's friends went there, and by this time we had another dog, she was a Golden Labrador. Oh she was 'ma lassie'. We trained her the same way as when we had Bruno. My dad would always say, "Mind I put the wee half teaspoon of olive oil in her dinner to keep her coat soft and shiny." She would always be at the door with my mum when I was coming home from work, and when she saw me her wee tail would be going like mad. We were both so happy to see each other. I would take her everywhere I went and we would go for long walks.

I will always remember that one time we were going for a walk, and my mum and dad smoked at the time, so my mum asked me to get her cigarettes when we were out. I did, but we were out walking for over an hour so when we got home my mum said,
"What kept you?"
I said, "We just went for a walk." And me, not realising that she really wanted them straight away. My mum said, "A walk? I've been waiting on you coming back for an hour and I've been waiting to have a cigarette."
She wasn't happy, so Goldie and I went up to my room. I'd listen to my music and Goldie would be lying on the bed. After a while we went downstairs for dinner, and I would give Goldie her dinner also, everything was okay. Well, after my mum had her cigarette, ha-ha.
So, I didn't do that again in a hurry. There was this one time Goldie and I went out for a walk and there were two police men coming towards us and they said, "That's a beautiful dog you've got,."
I said, " Aye, she's ma lassie."
And then they said, "Would you not like to give her to the police and we can train her for a police dog?"
I said, "No, she's she my dog and I'm not giving her away."
 So, we just carried on with our walk. But when we got home I was telling my mum and dad what the police asked, and my dad said, "Aye that will be right! She's not going anywhere. She was awesome. I would take her to the ice-cream van with me and get her a cone. My mum and dad always wanted a 'double nugget' and whatever I was buying for myself. We got to know the guy in the ice cream van as he was one of my older brothers mate. So, after I got everything I asked him how much is that, he said, "Goldie gets hers for nothing."
This happened all the time when I took her to the van. On a Friday we had the butcher van that would come, and when I was at work my mum would take Goldie with her to get her butcher meat. He also had a butcher's shop not far but he always came round on a Friday, and he would give Goldie a marrow bone. She loved it! I taught Goldie to 'give me a paw…to be a good girl', and then I would give her a treat. She used to lay in the garden when my mum would let her out, but then she went into the playground sometimes to lie on the grass. When the kids came out for their playtime

they all new Goldie and they would give her some sweets, and yip she loved getting pampered. There was this one time I can remember when I came home from work and Goldie was at the door with my mum. As usual she was so happy to see me, so when I went in I would go upstairs to get changed, and when I came back down my mum said, "Ask Goldie what she did today."
I said, "Oh', what did you do today? Were you a bad girl or a good girl"
Well, if she'd been 'a bad girl', she would turn her head away from you and if she'd been 'a good girl' she would put her paw on my knee, so this time she turned away and I said, "What did you do?"
My mum said she went down to the pensioners houses, and they all new Goldie also. They stayed at the end of the street, and one of the pensioners would bring her back after giving her something to eat. She would 'get a piece at anybody's door', as they say in Glasgow. She said to my mum, "She's had her dinner.'

There wasn't anywhere I went with Goldie that no one knew who she was. She was just so special and my best friend, but when she was about ten years old she took a cist in her right eye. The vet said that it would need to come out, so Goldie went into hospital for about a week. As none of the kids or the pensioners saw her about they came to the door to ask where she was, I said, "She's in hospital with a sore eye, and as soon as she comes home I will be out with her."
But at this point I didn't say what was really wrong so when Goldie came home she was a wee soul. I felt so sorry for her but it didn't hold her back from doing anything. But of course we had to be more careful,. When I was out with her some of the kids saw me with her and they came running up to see her. When they did and saw that she only had one eye, they said, "Aw what's happened to her eye?"
I explained to them what was wrong, and the kids said "Aw, that's a shame."

About two years later we lost Goldie to really bad arthritis and she could hardly walk. So, my dad and one of our neighbours took Goldie to the vet and he said, " The kindest thing we can do is to 'put her to sleep."
I broke my heart; it was so sad. My dad said that he'd never do that again because it was so hard and sad to see her go. We never got any more pets but I am still a great

animal lover. Now, I just pet-sit my friend's dog's and some of them it's cats, but not all at the same time.

I always remember that when we would have family parties when I was growing up we'd listen to all the music from the 60s that was played. It was amazing to listen to, Elvis, Tom Jones, Patsy Cline, Engelbert, Connie Frances, and lots more. I will always remember that my younger sister and me and my cousins were told to play in the room, because we were too young to be joining in when we had a party. So, we would have juice, sweets and crisps, and we would play games: we had snakes and ladders and Kerplunk and we would play 'eye-spy' with my little eye. We had a good laugh. When we would hear the music going off, it was time for a sing song, and we were allowed to come and listen to my mum, dad and everyone singing. I loved listening to my mum and dad singing; it was beautiful; they were brilliant. I will never forget that if anyone joined in, my dad would say, "One singer, one song."
I really loved to listen, to hear them all singing. When I got a bit older, at my secondary school, I would listen to my own kind of music. I began to play the records and record them all on to tapes and play them when we had a party. Or if it was at one of my aunties houses I would bring the tapes with me, and everyone enjoyed all the different kinds of music mixed on to the tape.It meant that we didn't have to put the records on because the tape was longer.

When my aunt and uncle would come up for a wee visit to see my mum and dad we would play with my cousins out in the back. There was a grass verge and we used to play football. So, when we came back upstairs and into the house to sit in the living room where my mum, dad and my aunt and uncle were, we would sit and listen. They would always be speaking about all sorts of different things. Mario was just a baby at the time. I can remember that I butted in to say something, that they were speaking about, and my dad said, "You should be seen and not heard, and to speak when you're spoken to.'
The adults were speaking, and the thing was I didn't realise it, but I certainly didn't do it again, because a telling off from my dad was enough. That was just the way adults and children related back then.

I bought a lot of music like tapes, and vinyl records when I started work. Cd's were not out at that time, as they didn't start to come out until the early eighties; that was when the first compact disc was manufactured.

It was brilliant when the compact disc came out. I then started to buy cd's and what a collection I started to collect. To this day I've still got them and a great collection.

My dad would go for a pint with some of his work mates on a Friday when they finished work, they had two pubs that they really liked going to, one of them was the Quarter Gill and other pub called the Dolphin. I will always remember one time when my dad came home, it was about after 10pm and he had 'a wee drink in him', so my mum would make my dad a couple of sandwiches. Well, my dad fell asleep so my mum said,

"That will get cold."

It was sausage and bacon, so we ate it and when my dad woke up about two hours later, he said to my mum,

"Did you make me something to eat?"

My mum said, "Aye, you ate it, and you drank half of your milk."

My dad said, " I can't remember."

My mum made my dad another couple of sandwiches, and we all had tea and sandwiches It was so funny though. And what beautiful memories I will cherish for ever.

Sometimes in life

I would like to share with you this beautiful Poem that my sister-in-law Pat wrote when my mum passed away. I think sometimes in life you can deal with anything Some issues can be hard, whether it be how big or small, the hardest thing though to deal with is when you lose your parents. I know everyone deals with grief in their own way, but it still doesn't make it any easier and you just carry on the best you can to get on with your life.

GIFTS FROM A MOTHER

Maria,   Gift number 1
Will now be the motherly one.

Tony,   Gift number 2
Her first-born son.

Alice,   Gift number 3
Her namesake.

John,   Gift number 4.
Well ! who could ask for more.

Margaret,   Gift number 5.
And mush more she is.

Roberta,   Gift number 6.
Another girl, it's time to quit.

Mario,   Gift number 7.
Oh, what a shock,
Last but not least.

Alice and Tony,
    Created a past, a family who will stand together as long as life will last.

Margaret Coletta is currently the Community Chef at Growing 21 Ltd in Ruchazie, Glasgow

Printed in Great Britain
by Amazon